Bicycles
by Design

Written by Jenny Feely

Series Consultant: Linda Hoyt

WorldWise
Content-based Learning

Contents

Introduction

The year without a summer

Over two hundred years ago, the quickest way to get from one place to another was to ride a horse. Then, in 1815, Mount Tambora, a volcano in Indonesia, erupted. It was the biggest **eruption** ever recorded on Earth. The ash and gases from the volcanic explosion filled the **atmosphere** and blocked sunlight from reaching Earth.

Even though the eruption happened in Indonesia, the effects were felt far away in Europe. The summer of 1816 was so cold, the crops would not grow. Without the crops, there was not enough hay for horses to eat. All over Europe, horses began to starve and die. Suddenly, getting from place to place was much harder.

Disaster sparks ideas

This disaster gave the German inventor Karl Drais an idea. He wondered if there could be another way for people to get around. And so he began to design, test and build the first bicycle.

On 12 June 1817, Drais took his invention for a ride. He travelled 12 kilometres in less than an hour. This was about the same speed as a horse trotting. Although it was an uncomfortable and dangerous ride, it was the start of a series of inventions that led to the development of the bicycles we ride today.

Karl Drais

Did you know?

Drais's invention was designed to be a horseless carriage. It was made of wood.

5

Chapter 1

Innovations

The hobbyhorse

The first bicycle built by Karl Drais was called the hobbyhorse.

The hobbyhorse was very different from modern bicycles. It had a wooden frame and wheels, but no **pedals** or brakes, and it was very heavy – it weighed over 20 kilograms. Riders sat on the saddle with their legs on either side, and used their feet to scoot along the ground and to stop. They used handles attached to the front wheel to **steer** the bike.

At this time, roadways had rough surfaces with many ruts and potholes. It was an uncomfortable surface for riders, so they rode on footpaths instead – a practice that was dangerous for **pedestrians**. In 1817, after a series of accidents, riding on footpaths was banned.

Did you know?

The hobbyhorse was also known as:

- a Draisienne (after its inventor Karl Drais)
- the velocipede (French for "swift walker")
- the Laufmaschine (German for "running machine")

The boneshaker

In 1866, a new bicycle design was developed. It had a metal frame and wooden wheels with iron tyres. It earned the nickname of the boneshaker because it was very uncomfortable to ride over the roads. To make the ride more comfortable, the seat was attached to the bicycle with a spring. Despite this, the rider felt every bump and jolt as they rode along. These bicycles could travel up to 12 kilometres per hour.

This bicycle was different from the hobbyhorse in one important way – it had pedals.

The boneshaker had pedals attached to the front wheel.

The penny-farthing

A Frenchman, Eugène Meyer, invented the penny-farthing in 1869. He worked out that if the front wheel of a bicycle was much larger than the back wheel, the bicycle would go faster. These bicycles were known by different names including the high wheeler, hi-wheel and penny-farthing. They had solid rubber tyres and brakes.

To get onto such a tall bicycle, a rider would put one foot on a peg sticking out of the back wheel and scoot along until the bicycle was moving. Then they would leap into the saddle – all the time trying to maintain the balance of the bicycle.

Using larger wheels enabled the penny-farthing to go faster, but this also made it more dangerous. Penny-farthing bicycles were used for races and could reach speeds of up to 40 kilometres per hour.

Did you know?

The penny-farthing got its name from two English coins of the time – the large penny and the much smaller farthing.

Did you know?

Thomas Stevens was the first person to ride a penny-farthing around the world. It took him from April 1884 to December 1886.

9

The safety bicycle

During the 1880s, the Rover safety bicycle was produced. Because this bicycle was lower and more stable than the penny-farthing, it was called the safety bicycle. Soon it was being copied by **manufacturers** all around the world.

The Rover safety bicycle looked a lot like the bicycles we ride today. It had a diamond-shaped metal frame. The pedals were placed below the seat, making pedalling easier and safer. The pedals were attached to the back wheel with a chain. This was the first bicycle to have **gears**, which enabled the rider to turn the back wheel more easily.

The safety bicycle was made of lighter, stronger metals and was easier to pedal.

Did you know?

Riders of high wheelers did not like the safety bicycle. They called them dwarf machines, crawlers and beetles.

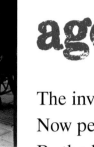

Chapter 2

The golden age of cycling

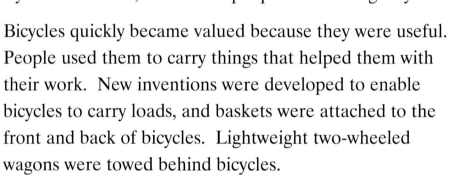

The invention of the safety bicycle changed the world. Now people could travel from place to place independently. By the late 1890s, millions of people were riding bicycles.

Bicycles quickly became valued because they were useful. People used them to carry things that helped them with their work. New inventions were developed to enable bicycles to carry loads, and baskets were attached to the front and back of bicycles. Lightweight two-wheeled wagons were towed behind bicycles.

The high demand for bicycles meant that many companies were set up to manufacture them. Bicycles became safer to ride as their brakes improved. They also became more comfortable – air-filled tyres replaced hard rubber tyres, and **shock absorbers** were added to the front and back wheels. Steering improved as the shape of handlebars changed. New and thinner materials were used for the frame, and **gears** were added. This made bicycles faster, lighter and easier to pedal.

Cycling changed women's lives

Bicycles changed women's lives. For the first time, women, too, could move from place to place easily and freely. At first, men thought that women would not be strong enough. But women rode their bicycles without difficulty.

Cycling changed women's fashion, too. Women had been wearing long skirts that were pulled in tightly around the waist. This way of dressing made it hard to breathe and did not suit cycling. Soon women began to ride in long pants, called bloomers, under shorter skirts.

"Let me tell you what I think of bicycling. I think it has done more to **emancipate** women than anything else in the world. I stand and rejoice every time I see a woman ride by on a wheel. It gives women a feeling of freedom and self-reliance."

Women's rights activist,
Susan B. Anthony, 1896

Chapter 3

Ever-changing bicycles

Today, advances in technology and science have improved the steering, safety, comfort and speed of bicycles. They have become lighter, stronger and faster. Different types of bicycles are designed to best suit the place where they are ridden.

Road bicycles

Road bicycles are designed for riding on paved surfaces. They have curled handlebars and thin tyres that make them faster at travelling on the road.

Mountain bicycles

Mountain bicycles are designed for rough mountain trails. They have strong frames and thick tyres that grip the ground and stop the bicycle from sliding. Many mountain bicycles have **shock absorbers** that soften the bumps and jolts from rough **terrain**.

Racing bicycles

Racing bicycles are designed to go as fast as possible. They are made from lightweight materials, have thin tyres, and can be raced on roads or on an indoor track. Track-racing bicycles don't have brakes. Instead, when the race is over, the rider lets the bicycle glide to a stop.

Recumbent bicycles

Recumbent bicycles have longer frames and a seat that is like a chair. These bicycles are more comfortable to ride and are often used by people who have back problems.

BMXs bicycles

BMX bicycles have small wheels and high handlebars, making it easy to turn them in small circles and lift them to do jumps. BMXs are used for fun, to race and to do tricks.

Did you know?

BMX stands for Bicycle motocross.

17

Bicycle safety

Bicycle safety has continued to improve over time. The invention of bicycle helmets has increased the safety of the rider if they have a crash.

Reflective materials on bikes and on cyclists' clothing, as well as the addition of lights, have improved safety when riding at night.

New brake materials and design have made stopping easier and safer – even in wet conditions.

The creation of separate bike paths has taken riders away from the dangers of riding on busy roads.

What to wear

- bright clothes
- helmet
- gloves
- shoes (closed toes)
- sunglasses

What to do

1. Make sure the brakes are working and that the tyres are pumped up.

2. Ride only on bike paths and in parks.

3. Watch out for other riders, **pedestrians** and dogs.

4. Brake early and slow down when you come to a corner.

5. Watch out for dangers such as low tree branches, potholes and wet or muddy patches.

6. Obey signs and warnings.

Bicycles today

Many people thought the invention and popularity of the motorcar would mean that bicycles would no longer be used. This has not been the case. Today, bicycles are used for business and pleasure.

Cars	Bicycles
Advantages	**Advantages**
Faster	Cheap to buy
More comfortable	Help physical fitness
Provide protection from the weather	Can go places that cars can't
Transport multiple people and big items	Do not cause air pollution
Disadvantages	**Disadvantages**
Expensive to buy and maintain	Slower
Cause air pollution	Not good for the very young or very old
	Not suited to long distances

Public bike sharing

Bike-sharing programs operate in many cities around the world. Locals or tourists can rent a bicycle and use it for as long as they need. These programs are good for the environment, convenient and help people keep fit.

Bicycles have been around for two hundred years. They are practical and fun to use. They will be around for a long time to come.

Conclusion

Tomorrow's bicycles

Since the first bicycle was invented in 1817, there have been many changes in the way bicycles look, what they are made of and how they are ridden. These changes have come about as people use their skill, creativity and knowledge to make bicycles stronger, easier to ride, faster and more comfortable. As new materials are invented, these also will become part of the story of the bicycle.

Glossary

atmosphere the air that surrounds the earth

emancipate to set free

eruption to come out in a sudden explosion

gears parts of a machine that control speed

manufacturers companies that make products

pedals flat pieces of metal that are pushed to make a machine work

pedestrians people who are walking

recumbent in a lying position

reflective to send back light from a shiny surface

shock absorbers devices that help reduce the impact of bumps and vibrations

steer to control the direction in which something moves

terrain a type of land

Index